PERSONAL TIME MANAGEMENT

Marion E. Haynes

CRISP PUBLICATIONS, INC.
Los Altos, California

PERSONAL TIME MANAGEMENT

Marion E. Haynes

CREDITS
Editor: **Michael G. Crisp**
Designer: **Carol Harris**
Typesetting: **Interface Studio**
Cover Design: **Carol Harris**
Artwork: **Ralph Mapson**

Copyright © 1987 by Crisp Publications, Inc.
Printed in the United States of America

English language Crisp books are distributed worldwide. Our major international distributors include:

CANADA: Reid Publishing, LTD., Box 7267, Oakville, Ontario Canada L6J 6L6. TEL: (416) 842-4428, FAX: (416) 842-9327

AUSTRALIA: Career Builders, P. O. Box 1051, Springwood, Brisbane, Queensland, Australia 4127. TEL: 841-1061, FAX: 841-1580

NEW ZEALAND: Career Builders, P. O. Box 571, Manurewa, Auckland, New Zealand. TEL: 266-5276, FAX: 266-4152

JAPAN: Phoenix Associates Co., Mizuho Bldg. 2-12-2, Kami Osaki, Shinagawa-Ku, Tokyo 141, Japan. TEL: 443-7231, FAX: 443-7640

Selected Crisp titles are also available in other languages. Contact International Rights Manager Tim Polk at (415) 949-4888 for more information.

Library of Congress Catalog Card Number 86-72076
Haynes, Marion E.
Personal Time Management
ISBN 0-931961-22-X

TYRANNY OF THE URGENT

Have you ever wished for a thirty-hour day? Surely this extra time would relieve the tremendous pressure under which we live. Our lives leave a trail of unfinished tasks. Unanswered letters, unvisited friends, unwritten articles, and unread books haunt quiet moments when we stop to evaluate.

But would a thirty-hour day really solve the problem? Wouldn't we soon be just as frustrated as we are not with our twenty-four allotment? A mother's work is never finished, and neither is that of any manager, student, teacher, or anyone else we know.

When we stop to evaluate, we realize that our dilemma goes deeper than shortage of time; it is basically the problem of priorities. Hard work does not hurt us. We know what it is to go full speed for long hours, and the resulting weariness is matched by a sense of achievement. Not hard work, but doubt and misgiving produce anxiety as we review a month or year and become oppressed by the pile of unfinished tasks. Demands have driven us onto a reef of frustration. We confess, quite apart from our sins, "we have left undone those things which we ought to have done; and we have done those things which we ought not to have done."

Several years ago an experienced manager said to me, "Your greatest danger is letting the urgent things crowd out the important." He didn't realize how hard his maxim hit. It often returns to haunt and rebuke me by raising the critical problem of priorities.

We live in constant tension between the urgent and the important. The problem is that the important task rarely must be done today, or even this week. The urgent task calls for instant action—endless demands, pressure every hour and day.

Even a home is no longer a castle; no longer a place away from urgent tasks because the telephone breaches the walls with imperious demands. The momentary appeal of new distractions seems irresistible and important, and they devour our energy. But in the light of time's perspective their deceptive prominence fades; and with a sense of loss we recall important tasks we have pushed aside. We realize we've become slaves to the "tyranny of the urgent."

Edited from: *Tyranny of the Urgent,* by Dr. Charles E. Hummell, InterVarsity Press, Downers Grove, IL., © 1967. Used by permission of the publisher.

PREFACE

This self-study book can help you become a better manager of time; however, it won't manage time for you. That is your responsibility. Effective time management is an experience in self-discipline, and you are the key to success. If you make use of the principles and techniques in this book, you will manage your time with less stress and accomplish more.

The objectives of this book are to:

- Help you determine how you presently use time.

- Make you aware of that portion of time over which you have control.

- Teach you how to make the most effective use of the time you control.

- Help you handle time not under your control in a more efficient way.

- Allow you to use time the way you choose (work, play or rest).

Those motivated to complete this book will gain from the experience. I hope you are one of them. Good luck.

Marion E. Haynes

CONTENTS

PART I
TIME MANAGEMENT PRINCIPLES

THE BASICS OF TIME MANAGEMENT

Time is a unique resource. Day to day, everyone has the same amount. It cannot be accumulated. You can't turn it on or off. It can't be replaced. It has to be spent at the rate of sixty seconds every minute.

Time management, like other management, benefits from analysis and planning. To understand and apply time management principles, you must know not only how you use time, but also what problems you encounter in using it wisely, and what causes them. From this base you can learn to improve your effectiveness and efficiency through better time management.

Time management is a personal process and must fit your style and circumstances. It takes a strong commitment to change old habits; however, this choice is available and yours for the taking. If you choose to apply the principles in this book, you will obtain the rewards that come from better time investment.

The questionnaire on the facing page will assist you in looking at your current time management attitudes and practices. It will help you identify the things you will want to concentrate on as you complete this book.

WE ALL GET 168 HOURS PER WEEK HOW DO YOU USE YOURS?

Place a check in the column that best describes how you feel or act. Then review your responses and focus on each item to see if it represents an opportunity to improve your management of time.

	Usually	Sometimes	Rarely
1. Do you normally spend time the way you really want to?	____	____	____
2. Do you often feel harried, and obligated to do things you really don't want to do?	____	____	____
3. Do you feel a sense of accomplishment from your work?	____	____	____
4. Do you work longer hours than your colleagues?	____	____	____
5. Do you regularly take work home evenings or weekends?	____	____	____
6. Do you feel stress because of too much work?	____	____	____
7. Do you feel guilty about not doing a better job?	____	____	____
8. Do you consider your job to be fun?	____	____	____
9. Can you find blocks of uninterrupted time when you need to?	____	____	____
10. Do you feel in control about the way you use your time?	____	____	____
11. Do you maintain a regular exercise program?	____	____	____
12. Do you take vacations or long weekends as often as you would like?	____	____	____
13. Do you put off doing the difficult, boring, or unpleasant parts of your job?	____	____	____
14. Do you feel you must always be busy doing something productive?	____	____	____
15. Do you feel guilty when you occasionally goof off?	____	____	____

Adapted from *Successful Time Management*, by Jack D. Ferner, pp. 6-7, New York, NY: John Wiley & Sons. © 1980. Used by permission of the publisher.

WHAT CONTROLS YOUR TIME?

The best starting place to improve your use of time is to determine the extent to which you control the time available to you. No one has total control over a daily schedule. Someone or something will always make demands. However, everyone has <u>some</u> control, and probably more than they realize.

Some time ("working hours" or "school hours") is regulated and should be used for those activities. Even within this structured time, there are opportunities to select which tasks or activities to handle and what priority to assign to that task. It is the exercise of these discretionary choices that allow you to control your time.

CONTROL OF YOUR TIME

As an employee, your scheduled work hours should be used in pursuit of company objectives. In school, your time should be spent studying and learning. To this extent, the use of your time is often controlled by specific tasks or assignments. However, several degrees of freedom usually exist in any specific time period. Where are you? (Circle one of the numbers below.)

I Have   10   9   8   7   6   5   4   3   2   1   0   I Have
Total Control   No Control

Tasks or activities which allow personal control of my time.	Tasks or activities which limit my control of time.
_____	_____
_____	_____
_____	_____
_____	_____
_____	_____
_____	_____
_____	_____
_____	_____
_____	_____

THREE TESTS OF TIME

> Although the examples described in this book are basically from the business world, similar principles apply to other aspects of your life.

Analyzing how you presently use time is the first step to achieving better control of it. You must have specific, reliable information before you can determine opportunities for improvement. The best way to gather information is to keep a time log. Instructions and forms for such a log are provided on page 55-57.

Once this information has been recorded, you should examine it from three points of view–necessity, appropriateness, and efficiency. This should allow you to discontinue certain tasks; delegate others; and/or find ways to increase efficiency through technology, new procedures, or personal work habits.

A careful analysis, can often earn you another eight to ten hours each week to spend on activities of your choice.

1. **The Test of Necessity:** First you should scrutinize each activity to be sure it is necessary–not just nice; but necessary. It is common to do things past their usefulness (i.e., monthly reports where the information is no longer used). This "test of necessity" should help reduce your tasks to the essential elements.

2. **The Test of Appropriateness:** Once the essential tasks have been identified, the next step should determine who should perform them (i.e., appropriateness in terms of department and/or skill level). There are probably activities that could be given to others. You may also find you are doing work beneath your skill level which can be easily reassigned.

3. **The Test of Efficiency:** The third analysis examines tasks that are remaining. Once satisfied you are doing necessary work you should, then ask: "Is there a better way?" This will encourage you to find a faster way using better technology or establish better procedures to handle recurring activities.

ANALYZE FOR EFFECTIVE TIME UTILIZATION

In your own words, and from your own situation, list opportunities for more effective use of your time using the three tests described on page 6.

The Test of Necessity: Following are my opportunities to eliminate some unnecessary tasks or activities:

_____

_____

_____

_____

The Test of Appropriateness: Following are opportunities to make better use of time by reassigning tasks or activities to others:

_____

_____

_____

The Test of Efficiency: Following are opportunities to become more efficient by using technology or developing better procedures:

_____

_____

_____

_____

There Are Only 3 Ways to Make Better Use of Your Time

1. Discontinue low priority tasks or activities.

2. Find someone else to take some of your work.

3. Be more efficient at what you do.

BENEFITS OF BETTER TIME UTILIZATION

When you are able to make better use of time, you can benefit from completion of longer term activities such as the following:

- **Career Planning:** Set a course for your future and lay out a plan to achieve it. Move to a proactive mode. Take charge of your own destiny.

- **Reading:** Staying current is increasingly important in today's complex world. More time will allow you to read job related materials; study new subjects; or learn more about a hobby or activity.

- **Communicating:** Extra time will allow you to improve and/or initiate interpersonal relationships.

- **Relaxing:** You need to plan time for relaxation. When you do not take time off from the daily grind your health may suffer, or you may "burn-out".

- **Thinking:** Improved methods and new opportunities come about as a result of innovation. More time will allow you to develop strategies and think through plans to establish and achieve significant new challenges. (Personal Performance Contracts by Roger Fritz listed in the back of the book is excellent for improving your job performance.)

CASE STUDY:
SHEILA LEARNS THROUGH EXPERIENCE

Three months ago Sheila looked forward to her promotion to supervisor. After four years in the department, she was confident of her abilities, and knew her staff was capable and experienced.

Today, Sheila isn't so sure she was cut out to be a supervisor. There seems to be no end to her workday. During office hours her day is filled assigning work and reviewing results. Also, there is a steady flow of visitors, and the phone rings constantly. In the evening, when she would like to relax, she has to take care of administrative matters such as reading mail, answering letters, preparing budgets and completing performance appraisals.

In frustration, Sheila asked her friend, Carol, to join her for lunch. Sheila said she had something important to talk about. At lunch, she told Carol she was thinking about giving up her supervisor's job. She said she just couldn't face a career of working 60 hours a week. Carol listened and then said there might be another way. If the only issue was the time required to do the job, perhaps a review of how Sheila was using her time might help. After listening to Sheila describe a typical week, Carol asked the following questions:

- Since she described her staff as "capable and experienced" why was Sheila spending so much time assigning work and review results?

- Who were the drop-in visitors? Could some be screened out?

- Could the department secretary take phone calls and refer some to others or have non-urgent calls returned at a more convenient time?

- Could some of Sheila's work be done by someone else?

With those thoughts in mind, Sheila returned to her office with a commitment to take a closer look at her use of time.

Consider Sheila's situation and, answer the following questions:

1. Does she appear to be making effective use of delegation? _____
   _____

2. If her visitors are employees, how might she avoid interruptions? _____
   _____

3. Should Sheila consider establishing a "quiet time" when she would receive no calls or visitors? If so, when might be the best time of day? _____
   _____

4. Sheila feels she should assign all departmental work and review all results. Is there a more efficient way? _____
   _____

5. What other ways could Sheila gain more control over her use of time? _____
   _____
   _____

HOW WOULD YOU HANDLE THESE SITUATIONS?

Listed below are situations where an opportunity exists to improve the use of time. Read each example and then check the choice you feel is the best response.

1. As Jean reviews time cards each week, she spends two hours summarizing the hours of employees who have exceptions such as sick relief or vacation relief. She is aware that the payroll department gathers this same information and provides it to all department heads. What should she do?

    ☐　a.　Continue summarizing the information.

    ☐　b.　Stop summarizing the information.

    ☐　c.　Point out the duplication to her supervisor and request permission to stop doing the work.

2. John likes to interview job candidates. He is excellent at matching candidates with job openings. Now that John is manager, he still spends about five hours a week interviewing even though he has a staff to handle this work. As a result, he often takes work home. What should John do?

    ☐　a.　Stay with his present practice. He's the manager and has the right to do as he wishes.

    ☐　b.　Delegate some of the administrative work to one of his staff so he can keep interviewing.

    ☐　c.　Stop interviewing except when the workload exceeds his staff's capacity.

3. When Gloria assumed her present job she noticed the quality of expense summaries she received from accounting was inadequate. Expenses were incorrectly allocated and often two months passed before accounts were correct. In order to have timely, accurate information, Gloria now spends six hours a week keeping her own records. What should she do?

   ☐ a. Continue keeping her own records. It is the only way to know they will be done correctly.

   ☐ b. Stop keeping her own records and use what the accounting department furnishes.

   ☐ c. Meet with the accounting department to work out a way to get the information she needs.

4. George is an assistant in the personnel department. Several times each month employees ask George to work up an estimate of their retirement benefits. He does each estimate by hand. Each estimate takes 45 minutes. What should George do?

   ☐ a. Continue his present practice. It seems to work okay.

   ☐ b. Refuse to prepare estimates except for employees planning to retire within one year.

   ☐ c. Develop and produce a computer generated summary sheet which can be personalized.

> The author feels the "c" choice is best in all situations.

PRIME TIME

When considering a daily schedule, it's a good idea to keep your energy cycle in mind. Some people are at their best early in the morning. Others peak in the afternoon. Whenever possible, try to plan your daily schedule to match your "prime time." You will not always have control but consider such ideas as reading, responding to mail or returning phone calls after lunch if your "prime time" is in the morning.

On the facing page is an exercise to help you visualize your energy cycle.

Typical Energy Cycle

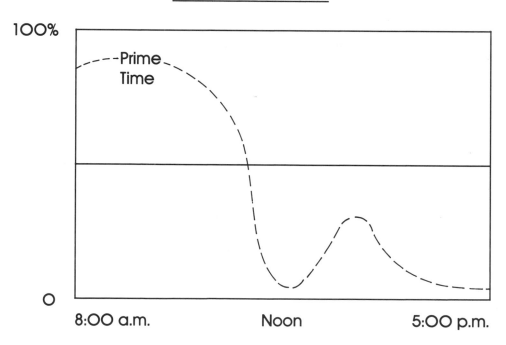

CHART YOUR ENERGY CYCLE

Fill in the beginning and ending time of your day on the following diagram. Then draw a line through the day reflecting your typical energy cycle.

100%

0

_____ A.M.   NOON   _____ P.M.

1. Do you arrange your workday (or class load) to take advantage of your energy cycle? _____

2. What could you do differently to better utilize your period of peak energy? _____

_____

_____

_____

SETTING PRIORITIES

When opportunities exceed resources, decisions must be made. Nowhere is this more apparent than in the use of time. Since time cannot be manufactured, you must decide what to do and what not to do.

Setting priorities in the use of time is a two-step process: (1) listing things that need to be done, and (2) prioritizing items on the list. (See facing page.)

Use the ABC method to determine your priorities by placing each item on your list into one of the following categories:

- Priority A–"Must-do": These are the critical items. Some may fall in this category because of management directives, important customer requirements, significant deadlines, or opportunities for success or advancement.

- Priority B–"Should-do": These are items of medium value. Items in this category may contribute to improved performance but are not essential or do not have critical deadlines.

- Priority C–"Nice-to-do": This is the lowest value category. While interesting or fun, they could be eliminated, postponed, or scheduled for slack periods.

Your A's, B's, and C's are flexible depending on the date your list is prepared. Priorities change over time. Today's "B" may become tomorrow's "A" as an important deadline approaches. Likewise, today's "A" may become tomorrow's "C", if it did not get accomplished in time and/or circumstances change.

Obviously, it is not worthwhile to spend considerable time on a task of modest value. On the other hand, a project of high value is worth the time invested. Only good planning will allow you to reap the benefits of time wisely invested.

Use the form on the facing page to practice setting priorities.

MY PRIORITIES FOR THE WEEK OF: _____

| Priority A—Must do |

_____

_____

_____

_____

_____

_____

| Priority B—Should do |

_____

_____

_____

_____

_____

_____

| Priority C—Nice to do |

_____

_____

_____

_____

_____

_____

(This sheet may be copied without further permission from the publisher.)

CRITERIA FOR SETTING PRIORITIES

- <u>Judgment</u>–You are the best judge of what you have to do. Let the pang of guilt you feel from not getting something done sharpen your judgment.

- <u>Relativity</u>–As you compare tasks or activities it should become clear that some are higher priority than others. You should always be guided by the question: "What is the best use of my time right now?"

- <u>Timing</u>–Deadlines have a way of dictating priorities. Also important, but often overlooked, is a required starting time in order to finish a project by deadline.

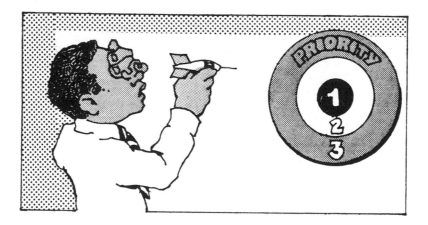

TWO HOURS A DAY

If you had 2 extra hours each day, how would you use them? Answer by putting an X in front of each statement that applies. Add your own ideas.

With 2 extra hours each day I would:

_____   1.   Do more planning.

_____   2.   Do more reading.

_____   3.   Spend more time on new work projects.

_____   4.   Spend more time with my family/friends.

_____   5.   Begin or expand an exercise program.

_____   6.   Spend more time on personal financial matters.

_____   7.   Start or expand a hobby.

_____   8.   (Add your own) _____

_____   9.   _____

_____   10.   _____

_____   11.   _____

_____   12.   _____

IN REVIEW

Reflect on the ideas presented thus far and consider the following:

- How much control do you have over the use of your time? How severely are you locked in by demands and deadlines? Do you exercise control when an opportunity presents itself?

- Within the time you control, are you doing only necessary and appropriate tasks? Are you doing them in the most efficient way?

- Do you know your energy cycle and can you make optimum use of your peak energy periods?

- Do you set priorities? Do you consistently handle your most important tasks first?

REVIEW WORKSHEET

1. Following are ways I can make better use of my time:

    _____

    _____

    _____

    _____

2. The major roadblocks to a more effective and efficient use of my time are:

    _____

    _____

    _____

    _____

3. If I ''find'' five hours a week, here is how I would use that time:

    _____

    _____

    _____

    _____

4. The following activities involve a lot of my time, yet don't seem to contribute to my objectives:

    1. _____

    2. _____

    3. _____

    4. _____

    5. _____

HOW TO CONTROL YOUR USE OF TIME

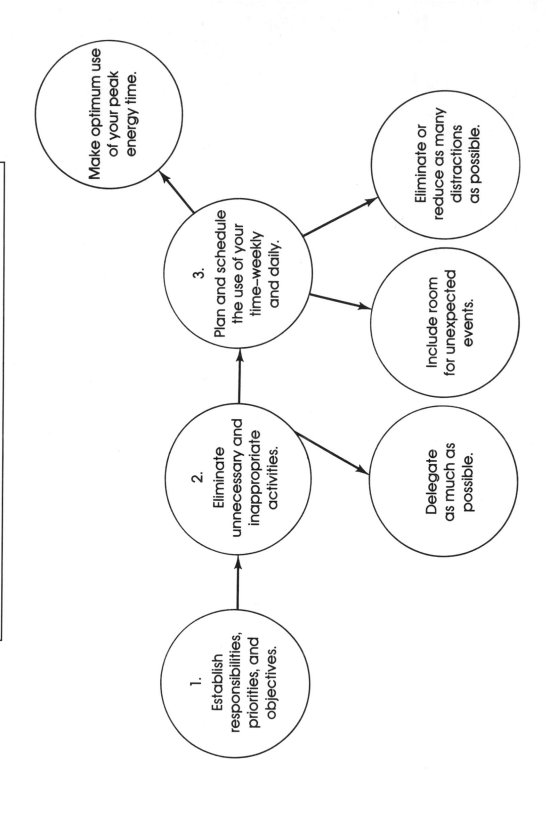

Make optimum use of your peak energy time.

3.
Plan and schedule the use of your time—weekly and daily.

Eliminate or reduce as many distractions as possible.

Include room for unexpected events.

2.
Eliminate unnecessary and inappropriate activities.

Delegate as much as possible.

1.
Establish responsibilities, priorities, and objectives.

PART I
SELF ASSESSMENT
QUESTIONNAIRE

The following statements summarize the principles presented in Part I of this book. Check those that apply to you. Review items you do not check to see if an opportunity may exist for future efficiency.

☐ I know when my peak energy period occurs.

☐ I have adjusted my daily routine to make maximum use of my peak energy.

☐ I have a written summary of my responsibilities.

☐ I have listed my objectives for the next quarter.

☐ I have prioritized my use of time.

☐ I have eliminated all unnecessary and inappropriate tasks.

☐ I have studied ways to improve efficiency in handling routine matters.

☐ I delegate whenever logical and possible.

☐ I plan what I want to accomplish each week.

☐ I prepare a daily "things to do list".

☐ I leave some time for the unexpected each day.

☐ I realize that I can't do everything and must choose the best alternatives.

PART II
TIME MANAGEMENT TECHNIQUES

PLANNING

Planning is a complex process. Some people are good at it, others aren't. Some seem so caught up in activities and deadlines they claim there is no time to plan. Yet, planning is the key to relieve the stress of too little time. It is the way to structure your future.

Planning makes two contributions which bring order to your life. First, it tells you how to get from where you are, to where you want to be. Second, it identifies the resources required to get you there. Through planning, you know when to begin something to complete it on schedule, and what it is going to cost.

Planning typically is either long-term or short-term. In this book, long-term plans describe what you expect to accomplish during the next three months as well as any project whose duration exceeds a week. Short-term plans cover what you expect to accomplish today or this week, although these may be steps toward longer term objectives.

MY TIME FRAME

- Long-term Objectives: Following are my objectives for the next quarter, plus my projects that will take longer than a week to complete:

_____

_____

_____

_____

_____

_____

- Short-term Goals: Following are those things that need doing this week (including steps toward longer term objectives):

_____

_____

_____

_____

_____

_____

TO REVIEW

Good Planning Includes:

- Establishing objectives

- Determining means and resources

- Assigning accountability (who will do what by when)

- Programming action steps

- Scheduling action steps

- Selecting start dates which allow completion of objectives by target dates

- Providing for measurement and review points

PLANNING AIDS AHEAD →

LONG TERM PLANNING AIDS

Planning aids are a critical part of effective time management. It simply is not possible to remember everything. Three common planning aids are presented on the following pages. These are an Action Planning Worksheet; a Milestone Chart; and a PERT Diagram. From these alternatives you can select the technique that best fits the type of work you do. Using a planning aid will help to bring order to your life.

One word of caution—don't get too elaborate. Don't spend more time drawing and updating planning aids than is required. In other words, your planning should save you time, not cost you time.

Regardless of the technique you choose, your master calendar should record all activities. Note the due dates for each action step, as well as the project completion date. When others are responsible for a step in your plan, ensure you have a follow-up date assigned. Also, always know who has responsibility for each step—and the date by when their action is to be completed.

CHOICES AVAILABLE

Long Term Planning Aids

- Action Planning Worksheet

- Milestone Chart

- PERT Diagram

- Master Calendar

ACTION PLANNING WORKSHEET

Action planning worksheets can vary greatly in their complexity. The simplist ones, show only those steps required to complete a project. Additional information (such as beginning dates, targeted completion dates, cost estimates, and who is responsible) can be added to the basic worksheet.

EXAMPLE

Action Planning Worksheet

Objective: *Publish a Work Planning and Review Workbook by May 31.*

Action Step	Est. Time	Target Date	Assigned Responsibility
1. Write draft	15 days	Apr. 15	Self
2. Type draft	10 days	Apr. 25	Secretary
3. Proofread	5 days	Apr. 30	Self & Secretary
4. Draw cover	5 days	Apr. 20	Graphics
5. Type Final	10 days	May 10	Key entry
6. Proofread	3 days	May 13	Self & Secretary
7. Make corrections	2 days	May 15	Key entry
8. Draw Figures	5 days	May 15	Graphics
9. Reproduce	15 days	May 30	Print shop
10. Deliver books		May 31	Print shop

ACTION PLANNING WORKSHEET

Objective: _____

_____

_____

_____

| Action Step | Target Date | Cost | | Assigned Responsibility |
		Dollars	Time	

(This sheet may be copied for your use.)

MILESTONE CHART

A Milestone Chart graphically displays the relationship of the steps in a project. To create one, list the steps required to finish the project and estimate the time required for each step. Then list the steps down the left side of the chart with dates shown along the bottom. Draw a line across the chart for each step starting at the planned beginning date and ending on the completion date of that step. Once completed, you should be able to see the flow of the action steps and their sequence (including those that can be underway at the same time).

The usefulness of a Milestone Chart will be improved by also charting actual progress. This is usually done by drawing a line in a different color under the original line to show actual beginning and completion dates of each step.

EXAMPLE

Objective: *Publish a Work Planning and Review Workbook*

by May 31.

Action Steps With Time Estimates:

1. Write draft	15 days	6. Proofread	3 days
2. Type draft	10 days	7. Make corrections	2 days
3. Proofread	5 days	8. Draw figures	5 days
4. Draw cover	5 days	9. Reproduce	15 days
5. Type final	10 days	10. Deliver books	

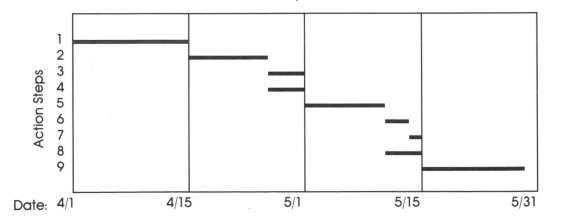

Action Steps

1
2
3
4
5
6
7
8
9

Date: 4/1   4/15   5/1   5/15   5/31

PRACTICE A MILESTONE CHART

Select a project and practice drawing a Milestone Chart.

Objective: _____

_____

_____

Action Steps With Time Estimates:

_____ _____ | _____ _____

_____ _____ | _____ _____

_____ _____ | _____ _____

_____ _____ | _____ _____

_____ _____ | _____ _____

_____ _____ | _____ _____

_____ _____ | _____ _____

_____ _____ | _____ _____

Action Steps

Dates

PERT DIAGRAM

PERT stands for Program Evaluation and Review Technique. It is a diagram that represents an added degree of sophistication in the planning process. To draw one, list the steps required to finish a project and estimate the time required to complete each step. Then draw a network of relationships among the steps. The number of the step is shown in a circle and the time to complete the step is shown on the line leading to the next circle. Steps that must be completed first are shown in order to clarify proper sequencing. Steps that can be underway at the same time are shown on different paths.

A PERT Diagram not only shows the relationship among various steps in a project, it also serves as an easy way to calculate the "critical path." The critical path is shown as a broken line in the example below. It is the longest time path through the network and identifies essential steps that must be completed on time in order to not delay completion of the total project.

EXAMPLE

Objective: *Publish a Work Planning and Review Workbook*

by May 31.

Action Steps With Time Estimates:

1. Write draft	15 days	6. Proofread	3 days
2. Type draft	10 days	7. Make corrections	2 days
3. Proofread	5 days	8. Draw figures	5 days
4. Draw cover	5 days	9. Reproduce	15 days
5. Type final	10 days	10. Deliver books	

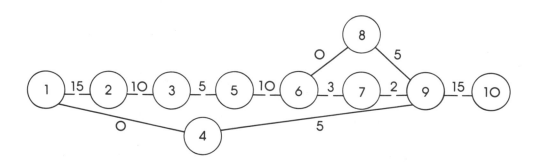

PRACTICE DRAWING A PERT DIAGRAM

Select a project and use it to practice drawing a PERT Diagram.

Objective: _____

_____

_____

Action Steps With Time Estimates:

_____	_____	_____	_____
_____	_____	_____	_____
_____	_____	_____	_____
_____	_____	_____	_____
_____	_____	_____	_____
_____	_____	_____	_____

(The usefulness of the PERT Diagram can be increased by coloring each step as it is completed. Actual time may be written over the estimated time to maintain a running tally of actual versus planned time along the critical path.)

SHORT-TERM PLANNING AIDS

Action steps in long-term plans must be integrated and prioritized with your other demands. These discrete steps become part of your short-term plans. Short-term plans are best developed and scheduled on both a weekly and daily basis.

<u>WEEKLY PLANS</u>

A weekly plan should describe what you want to accomplish by the end of the week, and the activities required to get you there. Weekly plans can be developed on Friday for the following week; over the weekend; or on Monday morning. (Many people use commute time for this activity.)

Weekly worksheets may be simple or complex. The example on the facing page can serve as a starting point for your short-term plans. You are free to copy and use this form.

Once completed, your worksheet should be kept handy for frequent reference. Daily activities should be transferred to a daily calendar, and take place according to an assigned priority.

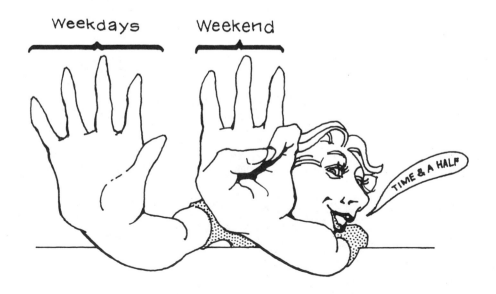

WEEKLY PLANNING WORKSHEET

For Week of: _____

Objectives:

1. _____

2. _____

3. _____

Activities	A/B/C Priority	Est. Time	Assigned Day

(This sheet may be copied for your use.)

DAILY PLANS

The culmination of the planning process is the best use of your time each day. If you make a habit of a daily calendar, many of your activities will already be recorded. This is the best starting place to develop your list of "things to do today."

A daily prioritized list is the best way to focus attention on your most important objectives. Work from the top of your list. If unexpected demands come up, assess their priority and handle them accordingly. Don't use something unexpected as an excuse to distract you. At the end of each day review what was accomplished and carry forward any items on your list that need completing. Reprioritize these with tomorrow's new items.

The format for your list is not important. It can be written anywhere–a calendar; a plain sheet of paper; or a form that you develop. Many stationery stores have a variety of planning forms available. The example below illustrates how simple a daily form can be. The example of the next page is more elaborate.

Use your "To Do" list to lay out a daily schedule. It should reflect meetings and appointments, plus time to accomplish other priority items on your list.

EXAMPLE

THINGS TO DO TODAY
Make travel arrangements
Attend budget review @ 10:00 a.m.
Complete salary proposals
Reserve conference room for Wed.
Call insurance agent
Make dentist appointment

DAILY PLANNING WORKSHEET

THINGS TO DO TODAY		
		Date:
Tasks to Complete	Done	Appointments to Keep
		7:00
		8:00
		9:00
		10:00
		11:00
		12:00
Phone Calls to Make	Done	
		1:00
		2:00
		3:00
People to See	Done	4:00
		5:00
		6:00
		7:00

(This sheet may be copied for your use.)

CONFERENCE PLANNER

Do you frequently need to communicate with co-workers for information to complete your work? Often, this causes an interruption they may find distracting. One way to handle the situation efficiently is to use a Conference Planner. (See the example on facing page.)

First enter the names of those you frequently call on. Then, as you think of an item you need to discuss, note it under the person's name. When it is time to have a conference, prioritize the list. Cross out unimportant items or those that can be handled better in some other way.

CONFERENCE PLANNER

Name:	Name:	Name:
Name:	Name:	Name:
Name:	Name:	Name:

(This sheet may be copied for your use.)

CHARACTERISTICS OF GOOD PLANNERS

The following statements describe how people view different aspects of planning. Check those statements which, in your opinion, reflect the views of a good planner.

- ☐ It is necessary to identify and operate within two time horizons. Anticipating events allows things to get done in the near term which contribute to achieving long-term objectives.

- ☐ An up-to-date master calendar can be your most helpful planning tool. However, detailed project plans must be developed before valid entries can be made on a master calendar.

- ☐ When things begin to get hectic, a "Things to do Today" list helps focus attention on the highest priority items.

- ☐ Action Planning Worksheets, Milestone Charts, and PERT Diagrams are excellent planning aids when properly used.

- ☐ Planning contact with colleagues and staff will help minimize the disruption of their schedules. One way to do this is to use a Conference Planner Worksheet.

- ☐ The most effective approaches to planning are those tailored to meet individual needs. Concepts, procedures, and worksheets are all subject to modification to fit individual circumstances.

CASE STUDY: ANOTHER DAY AT THE OFFICE

It was 7:20 a.m. when Myron arrived at the office. He was early because he wanted to clear the backlog of work that had been piling up on his desk. He turned on the lights and started to go through yesterday's mail. As he read the first piece, he realized he couldn't deal with it until a colleague arrived. He set it aside and went to the next. This item had potential application to a project he was working on, so he walked down the hall and made a copy for his personal use.

As he continued reading his mail he came across a journal article of particular interest and became engrossed in it. He was startled to find as he looked up that others were arriving and it was nearly 9:00 o'clock.

He quickly pushed the remaining mail to a corner of his desk and reached for a project file due tomorrow with at least two days' work yet to be completed. As he opened the file, Bill and Claire stopped by and invited him to join them for coffee. Myron decided he could spare ten minutes. Bill and Claire were both anxious to share the details of a play they attended last night. Before Myron realized it, thirty minutes had passed and he hurried back to his office.

As Myron entered his office, the phone rang. It was Mr. Wilson, his manager. There was a meeting scheduled at 10:00. Could Myron sit in for him? There was something to be discussed that the department should know about. Myron looked at his watch. There wasn't enough time to get started on the project so he pushed the file aside and vowed to start it immediately after lunch.

The afternoon wasn't any better. A few visitors, a few phone calls, a couple of letters and the day was over. Nothing had been accomplished on the project that was due tomorrow. As he stuffed papers into his briefcase, he wondered how Bill and Claire were able to attend plays during the evening.

Examine Myron's use of time:

1. Did he make good use of prime time? _____

2. Was he working on his highest priority task? _____

3. Did he seem able to say "No"? _____

4. Did he practice task completion? _____

5. Does he seem to understand his problem? _____

COMMON TIME WASTERS

Everyone wastes time. It's part of being human. Some wasted time can be constructive because it helps you to relax or otherwise reduce tension. Other wasted time, however, can be frustrating. This is especially true when time is wasted because you are doing something less important or less fun than what you might otherwise be doing.

The key question is what else might you be doing that is of a higher personal priority? Taking a break, communicating with associates, talking on the telephone, or reading are not time wasters unless they keep you from your primary objectives.

Time wasters usually result from two sources. One is environment, and the other is self. Some typical examples of each are shown on the facing page.

The next few pages in this book will concentrate on ways for you to recognize and manage your most frequent time wasters.

EXAMPLES OF COMMON TIME WASTERS

Self-Generated		Environmental	
	Page		**Page**
Disorganization	42	Visitors	46
Inability to Say No	44	Telephone Calls	46
Procrastination	44	Junk Mail	46
Lack of Interest (Attitude)	45	Waiting for Someone	47
Burnout	45	Unproductive Meetings	47
Others:		Crises	48
Gossip		Others:	
Unnecessary Perfectionism		Coffee Klatch Conversations	
		Unused Reports	

SELF-GENERATED TIME WASTERS

DISORGANIZATION: Disorganization is a key culprit for wasted time. Evidence of disorganization shows up in the layout of a work area. If time is spent searching for misplaced item; or wasted due to distractions which cause you to start and stop several times before a task is completed, then you need to evaluate your work area. Check it out. Is it efficient? Is it organized to minimize effort? Is there a free flow of materials and movement? Have you considered the placement of equipment such as telephone and calculator, the proximity of supplies that are frequently used, and your accessibility to active files?

Next, focus on your desk. Is your work area cluttered? How much time do you waste looking for things you know are there but can't find? When was the last time you used some of the items in and on your desk? Perhaps a housecleaning is in order.

The old axiom, ''A place for everything and everything in its place,'' is the best advice for organizing the information you need. Files should be set up for work in progress and kept handy. Everything relating to a particular project should be kept in one file folder. Files should be indexed for quick reference. Call-up procedures are required for items that need future action. A folder for current items received by mail, telephone, or visit should be maintained and checked daily to see what needs to be done.

Finally, organize your approach to work. Practice completing your tasks. If interrupted, do not immediately jump to a new task. First, assess the priority of a request, and avoid getting involved in any new activity until it becomes your top priority. If an interruption comes by phone or personal visit, simply return to the task you were working on as soon as the interruption ends.

HOW TO SET UP A PERSONAL FILE SYSTEM

* It is not necessary to be too logical. It is your system, and no one else will be using it so it only needs to make sense to you.

* Use a limited number of categories. For example, you may find the following 5 to be adequate:

  * Projects: In this category are individual files with information related to different projects you are working on.

  * Instant Tasks: This category should have folders on little jobs to fill in your time when you have a few minutes. Perhaps low priority letters to be answered, or general interest articles.

  * Self-Development: This category contains folders related to training: books, articles, etc.

  * Ideas: This category contains items you wish to investigate further to improve your operation.

  * Background Information: This category is a resource for various things you are involved with. Keep separate folders by topic and refer to them when you need statistics, examples, quotations, etc.

* It may be a good idea to color code by priority within each category to draw attention to your most important items. This is easily accomplished by using different color highlighters and marking individual folders.

* Keep your filing current so time won't be wasted searching for an item.

* Clean your files periodically to keep the volume of material to an essential minimum. This also will reduce time going through files when you are looking for something.

PROCRASTINATION: We all put things off. Typically, these items include boring, difficult, unpleasant, or onerous tasks that ultimately need completing. When this happens to you, consider the following ideas:

- Set a deadline to complete the task and stick with it.

- Build in a reward system. For example, tell yourself: ''When I finish that task I'm going to enjoy a nice meal with my special other.'' ''Or, I won't go home until I finish this task.''

- Arrange with someone (an associate, secretary, etc.) to routinely follow up with you about progress on tasks you tend to put off.

- Do undesirable tasks early in the day so you can be done with them.

Dealing With Procrastination

- ☐ Set a deadline
- ☐ Set up a reward system
- ☐ Arrange for follow-up
- ☐ Do it first
- ☐ Break job into small pieces
- ☐ Do it now!

INABILITY TO SAY ''NO'': At some point, we all have demands on our time which exceed our ability to accomodate them. Here is where learning to say ''No'' will come to the rescue. When you take on more than you can handle, your quality will suffer and you are better off to take on only what you can comfortably handle.

Saying ''No'' doesn't need to offend. One approach is to offer an alternative. Rather than saying ''Yes'' too often, try some of the following responses:

- ''I can take care of that but what I'm doing now will be delayed. Is your request more important?''

- ''I'll be glad to handle that for you. However, I can't get to it until I finish what I'm doing. That will be ....''

- ''I'm sorry I don't have time to take on any new work. I'll call you when my schedule frees up.''

- ''I appreciate your vote of confidence but just can't work it into my schedule at this time. Sorry.''

- ''I'm sorry, I just can't do it. Have you considered asking ...''

LACK OF INTEREST (ATTITUDE): If you waste time simply because of a lack of interest you should investigate alternatives that may be open to you. Some ideas are:

- Consider ways to make your work more interesting.

- See if you can swap tasks with a co-worker for better variety.

- Ask about reorganizing your work or sharing it.

- Reread the suggestions under procrastination.

- Read the book, *Attitude: Your Most Priceless Possession* by E.N. Chapman listed in the back of the book.

BURNOUT: If you waste time because you feel "burned out" you should consider some of the ideas presented above. If these do not work, arrange a counseling session with your manager to discuss how you are feeling and reasons that contribute to your "burnout". You should also read *Preventing Job Burnout* by Beverly Potter listed in the back of the book.

ENVIRONMENTAL TIME WASTERS

Even when you are well organized and making effective use of time, there will always be interruptions and distractions from outside sources. Here are ideas for handling some of the most common ones.

1. **VISITORS:** Controlling time taken up by visitors requires both courtesy and judgment. As a starting point, limit the number of people you invite to your work area. If you need to meet with a colleague at your facility, go to his or her work area. This way you can simply excuse yourself once your purpose is accomplished. It is often more difficult to get people to leave your area than it is for you to leave theirs.

Discourage drop-in visitors by turning your desk away from the door. When people see you are busy, they tend to not interrupt. Also, you might consider closing your door, (if you have one), when you need to concentrate.

When someone unexpectedly drops in, stand up to talk. Don't invite your visitor to be seated unless you have the time. Usually, when you stand, your visitor will also stand. This should shorten the length of the visit. If this does not work, be honest and say something like, "Thanks for dropping in. You'll have to excuse me now because I need to get this project finished."

2. **TELEPHONE CALLS:** For many, telephones are a constant interruption. You can't eliminate all of them. You can however limit the amount of time they take. If you are fortunate enough to have someone to answer your phone, calls should be screened. Review which calls need a personal follow-up, and delegate the others. Messages should be taken during periods when you do not wish to be interrupted.

When talking on the phone,* limit social conversation. Provide short answers to questions. End the conversation when it has achieved its business purpose in a polite way.

3. **MAIL:** A third distraction is your mail. Unsolicited mail arrives in an unending flood. If someone else sorts your mail, give some guidelines on what you want to see (separated in two piles, "information only" and "action"); what should be routed to others; and what should be tossed.

*(For an excellent book on telephone usage see: *Telephone Courtesy & Customer Service,* by Lloyd Finch listed in the back of the book.)

Learn to handle each piece of mail once. As you read it decide what action is required, and then take that action. (Even if it is to put it into an action file.) "Information only" mail can be saved and read at a more convenient time, (i.e., commuting, waiting for appointments, over lunch, in the evening, etc.).

You can save time by responding to some mail by telephone. If information is needed, it might be possible to have someone else telephone and pass on what is required.

Another idea is to write a brief response in longhand on the original letter and mail it back. If a record is needed, photocopy it before it is mailed.

4.   **WAITING:** We all spend too much time waiting—for appointments; for meetings to begin; for others to complete something; for airplanes; and as we commute. Opportunities exist to make better use of this "waiting" time.

Waiting need not be wasted time. Two approaches will help. First, don't spend unreasonable time waiting for others with whom you have appointments. If you go to someone's office and are not received promptly, leave word with a secretary to call you when your party is ready and return to your office.

The other way to make use of waiting time is to use it productively. For example, read your mail (including trade and professional journals); carry a tablet and pencil to develop plans or write letters; and/or carry a file of low priority items to complete.

A compact cassette recorder can help improve your productivity during travel and commuting. Either listen to information tapes, or use the machine to record ideas and instructions for when you return to your office.

5.   **MEETINGS:** Time wasted in meetings comes from two sources—the meetings you call, and the meetings you attend.

When you call a meeting, plan what you want to accomplish. Keep attendees to a minimum number of appropriate people. Briefly explain your agenda and move directly to the purpose of the meeting. Establish a time limit. Keep the discussion on track by periodically summarizing where you are. When the business has been completed, assign responsibilities, and establish follow-up dates to convert decisions to action, then adjourn the meeting.

A common time waster is the "regular staff meeting." Two suggestions can make significant improvements. First, set an agenda by asking, "What do we have to talk about today?" If more material is generated than can be handled in the available time, prioritize the list. If nothing significant is offered, adjourn the meeting. A second suggestion is to eliminate any discussion that involves only two participants. These should be handled as one-to-one sessions.

Before you attend someone else's meeting first make sure it is necessary for you to be there. If it is, arrive on time and prepared to participate in the discussion. Avoid taking the discussion off track and/or prolonging it. Work to make the meeting productive. Add any follow-up items to your list of things to do within appropriate priority designation.

6.   **CRISES:** Many people believe crises are unavoidable. That's only partly true. Unexpected events do occur which must be handled then and there. Many crises however are recurring events brought on by something that either was or was not done. When you delay something that needs doing, you are helping create a future crisis.

A starting point to reduce future crises is to review past crises. Are there patterns? Often, you can develop a response to recurring problems. For example, if there has been a regular breakdown of a particular piece of machinery, you can plan to respond to the next breakdown by replacement, having a standby available, etc.

Another way to reduce crises is through contingency planning. Study the key elements of a project (quality, quantity, cost, and timeliness), and think through three questions so you will be ready to respond when a crisis occurs:

- What is likely to go wrong?

- When will I know about it?

- What will I do about it?

Some crises are beyond your control. For example, you may have unrealistic deadlines laid on you; priorities may be changed at the last minute; people will make mistakes; machines will break down; etc. When this happens, take a deep breath, and relax for a few minutes. Think through what needs to be done and consider the alternatives. Then, approach the situation in an orderly, methodical way. You don't want to precipitate a second crisis simply trying to handle the first one.

WHEN THINGS GO WRONG

1. Renegotiate: The simplest action when you can't make a deadline is to renegotiate the due date. Perhaps there is enough flexibility that a day or two longer doesn't really matter. (See *Successful Negotiation* by Robert B. Maddox listed at the back of the book on how to handle this).

2. Recover Lost Time During Later Steps: If, in the early stages of a project, a step takes longer than planned, reexamine time allocations for the remaining steps. Perhaps other time can be saved so that overall time on the project will not increase.

3. Narrow The Scope of The Project: Once underway you may find it will take longer than planned to accomplish everything you planned. When time is critical, you may have to eliminate some non-essential things to meet the deadline.

4. Deploy More Resources: You may need to put more people or machines on the project. This option clearly increases the cost so it represents a decision choice of weighing the cost against the importance of the deadline.

5. Accept Substitutions: When a needed item is not available, you may be able to substitute a comparable item to meet your deadline.

6. Seek Alternative Sources: When a supplier you are depending upon cannot deliver within your time frame, look for other suppliers who can. (You may choose to pursue other sources before accepting substitutions).

7. Accept Partial Delivery: Sometimes a supplier cannot deliver an entire order but can deliver the amount you need to get you passed a critical point. After that, the remainder of the order can be delivered to everyone's satisfaction.

8. Offer Incentives: This option calls for going beyond the terms of an agreement to get someone you are dependent upon to put forth extra effort. It might be a bonus clause in a contract for on-time delivery, or a penalty clause for late delivery, or simply buying someone lunch to put forth an extra effort.

9. Demand Compliance: Sometimes it is necessary to stand up for your rights and demand deliverance according to the agreement. Occasionally, an appeal to higher authority will produce the desired results.

DEALING WITH YOUR TIME WASTERS

Now that you have read about time wasters and how to deal with them, take a few minutes to look at your own situation. List as many time wasters you have experienced as you can. Then, select the three most serious and consider ways to deal with them.

List of Time Wasters

Self-Generated	Environment

1. From your list of time wasters select the three most serious. What are they? How much time do they consume? What causes them?

    1. _____

    _____

    2. _____

    _____

    3. _____

    _____

2. List possible ways to reduce the impact of these time wasters.

    _____

    _____

    _____

CASE STUDY: THE PROGRAM REALLY WORKS

I have always admired how Bill does so much without seeming rushed. He always seems to have plenty of time when we talk. I know for a fact he rarely takes work home with him. I finally decided to ask Bill the secrets of his time management.

He began by saying he once had a real time management problem. Because of it, he looked for ways to make better use of time. He read books on the subject and put some of their ideas in practice. Bill explained that the most important lesson he learned was to adapt techniques to his individual situation. Bill explained the following four basic concepts as keys to his success:

First, and most important, Bill said he always looks ahead. He lists the goals he is working toward, and has a plan to get there. He said he has learned to anticipate when things are due without waiting to be asked. As an example, budgets are due the second quarter every year. Bill does not wait until he receives a memo requesting his budget, rather he works it into his schedule.

Second, he establishes priorities. There is always more to do than the time to complete it. Occasionally this may mean foregoing something he would like to do in favor of something that has to be done. When setting priorities, Bill said he takes into account his management's wishes as well as his judgment.

Third, Bill indicated he learned to not try to do everything himself. He relies on his staff. Bill knows the people he can depend on and lets them do their job. He also trains others until he can rely on them.

Finally, he said, use only those techniques that help you. For example, he said he doesn't make a ''Things To Do'' list most days, because often his days are routine. However, when things begin to pile up, he always makes a list and starts at the top.

CASE STUDY NUMBER THREE (Continued)

According to Bill, that's it. Four basic ideas to help get better control over time: (1) know your calendar; (2) prioritize demands on your time; (3) utilize the skills of others, and (4) use techniques that help your unique situation.

1. Do you think Bill's superiors see him as a good manager and why?

    _____

    _____

    _____

    _____

2. How do you think Bill's staff feel about working for him and why?

    _____

    _____

    _____

    _____

3. What do you learn from Bill's approach that could help you?

    _____

    _____

    _____

    _____

SIX TIPS FOR EFFECTIVE TIME MANAGEMENT

1. List and prioritize weekly objectives.

2. Make a daily "To Do" list and prioritize it.

3. Devote primary attention to your A's.

4. Handle each piece of paper only once.

5. Continually ask: "What is the best use of my time right now?"

6. Do it!*

*"The best way to begin, is to begin."

Marie Edmond Jones

PART III
ACTION PLANNING

APPLYING WHAT YOU'VE LEARNED

This section contains worksheets which will help you apply time management principles and techniques to your own situation. To complete this section, you need to do the following:

1. Gather Data: Keep a daily time log for one week similar to the one shown on pages 56 and 57. This will provide accurate information for you to improve your use of time. Be honest . . . and attentive to detail.

2. Analyze Your Use of Time: Working with the data gathered, analyze your current use of time. List opportunities for improvement.

3. Action Plan: From your analysis, develop specific action plans to bring about the desired improvement in your use of time.

4. Follow-up: Six weeks after beginning your time management improvement effort complete the Progress Survey shown on page 65 to assess your progress, and determine what work still needs to be done.

Instructions For Keeping Daily Time Log

- Select a typical week (i.e., avoid vacation, sick leave, personal leave, holiday, etc.)

- Record activities at least every half hour. Be specific. For example, identify visitors and record duration and topics of conversations. (Be honest. Only you will have access to this information.)

- Write a comment on each activity. Did something take longer than usual? Why? Were you interrupted?

- At the end of the day note whether this day was typical, busier than usual, or less busy than usual. Add up time spent in various major activities (meetings, visitors, telephoning, mail, etc.), and show totals along with other comments at the bottom of the Daily Log.

(See next two pages for sample Daily Time Log.)

56

(NOTE: Photocopy this form for each day of the week.)

DAILY TIME LOG	
Day Of Week: M T W T F	Date:
Time Activity	Comments
7:00	
7:30	
8:00	
8:30	
9:00	
9:30	
10:00	
10:30	
11:00	
11:30	
12:00	
12:30	
1:00	
1:30	
2:00	
2:30	
3:00	
3:30	
4:00	
4:30	
5:00	
5:30	

Was this day: _____ Typical?   Comments: _____

_____ More busy?   _____

_____ Less busy?   _____

(NOTE: Photocopy this form for each day of the week.)

DAILY TIME LOG		
Day Of Week: M T W T F		Date:
Time Activity		Comments
7:00		
7:30		
8:00		
8:30		
9:00		
9:30		
10:00		
10:30		
11:00		
11:30		
12:00		
12:30		
1:00		
1:30		
2:00		
2:30		
3:00		
3:30		
4:00		
4:30		
5:00		
5:30		

Was this day: _____ Typical?   Comments: _____

_____ More busy?   _____

_____ Less busy?   _____

TIME ANALYZER

Use your time log as a basis. Draw conclusions and record your response to the following questions.

1. Which part of each day was most productive? Which was least productive? Why?

   _____

   _____

   _____

   _____

   _____

   _____

   _____

   _____

2. What are the recurring patterns of inefficiency? (i.e., waiting for something, searching for something, interruptions, etc.).

   _____

   _____

   _____

   _____

   _____

   _____

   _____

   _____

3. What do you do that may not be necessary? (Be liberal since this list is simply for further review later).

_____

_____

_____

_____

_____

_____

4. What do you do that may be inappropriate? (Again, these are only prospects for further scrutiny).

_____

_____

_____

_____

_____

_____

5. Where are your opportunities for increased efficiency?

_____

_____

_____

_____

_____

6. What occasions do you allow enjoyment to override a priority task?

_____

_____

_____

_____

_____

_____

_____

7. Which activities do not contribute to achieving one of your objectives? How can you change this?

_____

_____

_____

_____

_____

_____

_____

8. On average, what percentage of work time are you productive? (Be honest). What is your reaction to this figure?

_____

_____

_____

_____

_____

_____

_____

PLANNING FOR IMPROVED TIME UTILIZATION

Step 1 | State your time improvement objective? Be specific both in terms of how much time you hope to free up in your weekly schedule and the target date by which you hope to accomplish it.

_____

_____

_____

Step 2 | Identify your areas of opportunity? Be specific. What tasks might be eliminated or reassigned? What time wasters can be eliminated or reduced? What planning needs to be done?

Opportunity   Estimated Time
                                                  Savings

_____   _____

_____   _____

_____   _____

_____   _____

_____   _____

_____   _____

_____   _____

_____   _____

_____   _____

_____   _____

Step 3 Select those opportunities you plan to pursue. Add up the anticipated time savings and compare it with your targeted time savings. (Space is provided for planning three opportunities. If you have more, photocopy as many additional pages as you need).

Opportunity No. 1: _____

_____

_____

Action Steps	Target Dates

Opportunity No. 2: _____

_____

_____

Action Steps	Target Dates
_____	_____
_____	_____
_____	_____
_____	_____
_____	_____
_____	_____
_____	_____

Opportunity No. 3: _____

_____

_____

Action Steps	Target Dates
_____	_____
_____	_____
_____	_____
_____	_____
_____	_____
_____	_____
_____	_____

64

Step 4

> List others who need to be involved when implementing your changes. This should include review and approval by your manager, as well as the agreement and cooperation of those who may assume part of your duties and/or responsibilities.

Supervisor: _____

_____

_____

_____

_____

_____

Associates: _____

_____

_____

_____

_____

_____

Staff: _____

_____

_____

_____

_____

_____

Step 5 | Follow up in 30 days. Review your progress and repeat any steps that have not provided the results you anticipated.

NOTES _____

_____

_____

_____

_____

_____

_____

_____

_____

_____

_____

PROGRESS SURVEY

Instructions: Six weeks after beginning your time management improvement effort complete the following survey. It will show where you are doing well, and where you still need to devote attention.

Scoring key: Yes—"1"; Usually—"2"; Sometimes—"3"; Rarely—"4"; Never or No—"5"; Not Applicable—NA.

1. Do you have a clearly defined list of written objectives? _____

2. Do you plan and schedule your time on a weekly and daily basis? _____

3. Can you find large blocks of uninterrupted time when you need to? _____

4. Have you reduced or eliminated recurring crises from your job? _____

5. Do you refuse to answer the phone when engaged in important conversations or activities? _____

6. Do you use travel and waiting time productively? _____

7. Do you delegate as much as possible? _____

8. Do you prevent your staff from delegating their tasks and decision making to you? _____

9. Do you take time each day to think about what you are doing relative to what you are trying to accomplish? _____

10. Have you eliminated any time wasters during the past week? _____

11. Do you feel in control of your time? _____

12. Is your desk and office well organized and free of clutter? _____

13. Have you reduced or eliminated time wasted in meetings?   _____

14. Have you conquered your tendency to procrastinate?   _____

15. Do you carry out work on the basis of your priorities?   _____

16. Do you resist the temptation to get overly involved in non-   _____
    productive activities?

17. Do you control your schedule so that others do not waste   _____
    time waiting for you?

18. Do you meet your deadlines?   _____

19. Can you identify the critical few tasks that account for the   _____
    majority of your results?

20. Are you better organized and accomplishing more than   _____
    you were six weeks ago?

21. Have you been able to reduce the amount of time you   _____
    spend on routine paperwork?

22. Do you effectively control interruptions and drop-in   _____
    visitors?

23. Have you mastered the ability to say "No" whenever you   _____
    should?

24. Do you stay current with your most important reading?   _____

25. Did you leave enough time for yourself—recreation, study,   _____
    community service, family?

TOTAL   _____

Scoring: Add the points assigned to each item. The lower your score, the better. Look particularly at items you rated "4" or "5". These represent challenges for further development.

This survey should be retaken quarterly as old habits have a way of recurring.

Adapted from *The Time Management Workbook*, by Merrill E. Douglas, Time Management Center, Grandville, MI, p. 16, © 1982. used by permission of the author.

PART IV
CONCLUSION

Congratulations on completing this program . . . we hope it was an effective use of your time!

Nearly everyone has the potential to save five to ten hours a week. To do so, requires discipline and a commitment to the basic principles in this book.

TIME MANAGEMENT IN A NUT SHELL

In review, you need to identify that portion of time over which you have control. Then develop procedures for repetitive operations and/or make use of available technology. You should concentrate on high pay-off activities.

Also, identify and make best use of your personal energy cycle. Use prime time to handle work requiring concentration. If possible, arrange for a quiet period to match your prime time when there are pressing matters.

Next, establish quarterly objectives and construct plans to accomplish them. Maintain some flexibility to respond to unexpected events. Prioritize the action steps required to achieve your objectives.

TIME MANAGEMENT IN A NUT SHELL (Continued)

Analyze your use of time. Keep a time log for a typical week, then examine your activities using the tests of necessity, appropriateness, and efficiency. From this examination determine the essential elements of your job and isolate time wasters and deal with them.

Finally, remember that the ideas in this book must be adapted to fit your unique situation. Modify the worksheets if necessary; develop your own personal file system; and use the planning techniques when appropriate. Don't let the use of forms and procedures distract you from doing your job.

Keep this program handy as a reference. To check your progress, make a note to review the book again in three months.

Good luck!

NOTES

FOR OTHER FIFTY-MINUTE SELF-STUDY BOOKS
SEE THE BACK OF THIS BOOK.

NOTES

FOR OTHER FIFTY-MINUTE SELF-STUDY BOOKS
SEE THE BACK OF THIS BOOK.

NOTES

FOR OTHER FIFTY-MINUTE SELF-STUDY BOOKS
SEE THE BACK OF THIS BOOK.

ABOUT THE FIFTY-MINUTE SERIES

We hope you enjoyed this book and found it valuable. If so, we have good news for you. This title is part of the best selling *FIFTY-MINUTE Series* of books. All other books are similar in size and identical in price. Several books are supported with a training video. These are identified by the symbol **V** next to the title.

Since the first *FIFTY-MINUTE* book appeared in 1986, more than five million copies have been sold worldwide. Each book was developed with the reader in mind. The result is a concise, high quality module written in a positive, readable self-study format.

FIFTY-MINUTE Books and Videos are available from your distributor or from Crisp Publications, Inc., 95 First Street, Los Altos, CA 94022. A free current catalog is available on request.

The complete list of *FIFTY-MINUTE Series* Books and Videos are listed on the following pages and organized by general subject area.

CUSTOMER SERVICE/SALES TRAINING (CONT.)

SMALL BUSINESS/FINANCIAL PLANNING

ADULT LITERACY/BASIC LEARNING

CAREER BUILDING

To order books/videos from the FIFTY-MINUTE Series, please:

1. **CONTACT YOUR DISTRIBUTOR**

   or

2. **Write to Crisp Publications, Inc.**
   95 First Street   (415) 949-4888 - phone
   Los Altos, CA 94022   (415) 949-1610 - FAX